FIESTA
XR2 & XR2i

FIESTA
XR2 & XR2i

The Enthusiast's Small Ford

Martin Lambert

Windrow & Greene

Published in Great Britain 1991 by
Windrow & Greene Ltd
5 Gerrard Street
London W1V 7LJ

British Library Cataloguing in Publication Data
Lambert, Martin
   Fiesta XR2 and XR2i: the enthusiast's small Ford.
   I. Title
   629.2222

ISBN 1-872004-41-5

Design: *ghk* DESIGN

Printed in Singapore by Craft Print

Contents

Acknowledgements

The author and publisher gratefully acknowledge the valuable assistance of the following in producing this book:
Dennis Foy, editor of *Performance Ford* magazine; Les Gent, of the XR Owners Club; Ford Photographic; Paul Newton (Panique); David Power (Power Engineering); Bill Blydenstein (Blydenstein Racing); Abbott Racing; Ian Shaw; Ian Wagstaff; Paul Cooper; Gary Kay.

The XR2: origins and arrival

Since the early 1980s, the Fiesta XR2 and, more recently, the XR2i have been providing one particular section of Ford's enormous clientele with just the sort of car they want — sporty in its handling and performance yet still civilised and practical, stylish, compact but not cramped, inexpensive to run but not austere. There wouldn't, of course, have been an XR2 at all if there hadn't been a Fiesta. So to understand how the XR2 came into being, we need to look first at the Fiesta in general. Familiar a part of the motoring scene though it may have become in the years since it first appeared, it was very much a new departure for Ford.

Before the introduction of the Fiesta in 1976, the party line had always been, 'Ford don't make small cars'. The company's identity as a household word almost world-wide derived from a history of mass-producing simple, rugged cars to meet the popular need for reliable, low-cost transport, a style that had been set right back at the beginning with the legendary Model T. Despite the success of one or two tiny cars, like the Austin Seven, Ford believed, and continued to prove for many years, that their purpose and that of their customers was best served by avoiding the ultra-light, minimal-motoring school of design.

That principle continued to guide them in the early postwar years. Through the 1950s and 1960s, Ford's argument was that cars like the Anglia and Escort, designed along well established conventional lines, one category smaller than the by now clearly defined medium-sized family saloon class, provided the best balance between cost and practicality. There was also a strong feeling within the company, borne out by the financial struggles of some of their rivals, that small cars didn't make money. It was a policy they clung to with a cautiousness that began to border on the stubborn.

The result was that by the early 1970s, there was an important sector of the market, particularly in Europe, in which Ford, despite being a major force on the car-manufacturing scene, did not have a contender. The bubble cars and micro-cars of the 1950s had proved to be a passing phenomenon, but the 'think *really* small' philosophy they embodied was a significant factor in the emergence of a much more enduring design, the BMC Mini. It's easy now to forget the impact that revolutionary little car had after its introduction in 1959. With the lofty wisdom of hindsight, we can say that the Mini, like many earlier baby cars, was still probably a bit *too* small (certainly, it seems clear that, as the sceptics in Ford predicted, it never did much for its manufacturer's profitability), but what it did in a big way was to change in a positive direction public perceptions about cars at the lower end of the size range, preparing the market for a whole generation of just slightly larger front-wheel-drive cars which were often defined, by reference to their illustrious predecessor, as the 'superminis'. Cars like the Datsun 100A Cherry, introduced in 1970, the Fiat 127 (1971), the Renault 5 (1972) and the VW Polo (first seen as the Audi 50 in 1974) quickly established their popularity and sold in numbers Ford could no longer ignore.

Another influence on the hierarchy of an American-based corporation was that the later 1960s had seen imported cars begin to make a big impact in the USA, so that thinking in terms of smaller and more compact vehicles became a more familiar activity. Europe was becoming more important to Ford, too: the British subsidiary became wholly owned in 1960 (the American

Above: The Fiat 127 was one of the cars which helped to establish the 'superminis' as an important element in the European car market, and Ford engineers examined it very closely when they were drafting the Fiesta.
Below: The VW Polo was a later entry to the ranks of the 'superminis' and it too came under scrutiny from Ford. Like the Fiat 127, it was a three-door hatchback of compact dimensions with a transverse engine driving the front wheels.

parent company had previously held less than 60%) and by 1967 Ford of Europe had been set up to integrate and rationalise production and development, bringing to an end the situation where Ford in Germany designed and built a different range of models from Britain. By the early 1970s, Ford was Europe's third largest car producer, equal with Renault, behind VW and Fiat. Against this background, the argument within Ford in favour of a new small car gained momentum and in 1973 'Project Bobcat', as it was called, got the final go-ahead.

As the project developed, it became clear that it would be much more of a 'clean-sheet-of-paper' job than most Fords tended to be. The evolutionary process, by which many engineering features and actual components of an earlier model were carried over into the next, even if the external styling effectively disguised them, was not going to be appropriate this time. Prototypes which tried to use existing elements pared down to suit the new baby — the rear-drive, live-axle layout of the Escort, for example — were just not acceptable either at the 'customer clinics' which Ford often used to gauge public taste or in the rigorous cost analysis which was applied to ensure profitability. The need for optimum space utilisation in a car of this size, as well as the improving standards of ride and handling which the market demanded, made front-wheel drive virtually obligatory. That was something Ford had only limited experience of, with the none-too-successful Taunus 12M, and it meant developing a new gearbox too. The well established opposition was setting the standard to a large extent, and Ford engineers paid very careful attention to their rivals' existing designs in the 'supermini' class. The Fiat 127, in particular, came under scrutiny, and early prototypes of the new car's mechanical components were road-tested by grafting them into Fiat bodyshells.

Below: The basic Fiesta followed the established 'supermini' formula very closely. It was a neat, simple design which sold well.

Above: The first sign of a sporty interest in the Fiesta range came with the S version, for which options included alloy wheels and a 1,300cc engine.
Below: This is the interior of the Fiesta S, with a rev counter incorporated in the instrument panel and bright striped upholstery.

Underbonnet view of the Fiesta 1300S shows the offset mounting of the Kent-derived OHV engine and the in-line position of the gearbox. Also visible is the transverse linkage between the brake pedal and servo which was necessary on right-hand-drive cars. The 1,600cc engine, when it arrived, was very slightly taller but not otherwise larger in its external dimensions.

Late in the project, the VW Polo became the main focus of comparison.

So the car which emerged at the end of a thorough process of development and rigorous durability testing had little in common with other Ford models. The engine was a version of the four-cylinder OHV Kent series familiar in Escorts and Cortinas, but it was mounted transversely (as in the Fiat and the VW), and almost everything else was new. It was to be built in a brand-new plant, too, at Almusafes near Valencia in Spain, on a 'green-field' site which had previously produced oranges, onions and artichokes. That was the original plan, anyway: in the event, identical cars were also made at Saarlouis and later Cologne in West Germany and at Dagenham in England. The gearboxes would come from the Ford transmissions plant at Bordeaux in France.

The Fiesta went on sale in Europe in 1976. A 'Federal' version for export to the USA, part of the same development programme, followed soon after, something which would later be of significance in the XR2 story. The car quickly established itself in the market-place. Competitively priced, cheap to run (low servicing costs had been a specific design aim) and available with a range of trim and equipment options, it did more or less just what Ford had hoped it would. For the real car enthusiast, though, it wasn't terribly exciting — a competent shopping trolley, but not much more.

Ford, of course, were past masters at producing that sort of car, calculated to appeal to the widest public, including the all-important fleet market.

Above: This Fiesta 1.1S has the 'Series X' additions — wider alloy wheels, wheelarch spats and spoiler — which were available from Ford dealers. — Below: The Supersport was a limited-edition Fiesta which had the 1,300cc engine, 'Series X' wheels, spats and spoilers, and shaded bodyside decals to create the illusion of flared wings. It prefigured the XR2 in some but not all details.

Above: This German equivalent of the Supersport had prominent '1300S' decals and added sill extensions to the body kit, something which was not at first carried over into the XR2. — Below: Cutaway drawing of a Fiesta with Ghia or S-style alloy wheels shows all the fundamental features of the design which were inherited by the XR2. Note the fuel tank mounted well forward out of harm's way under the rear seat pan.

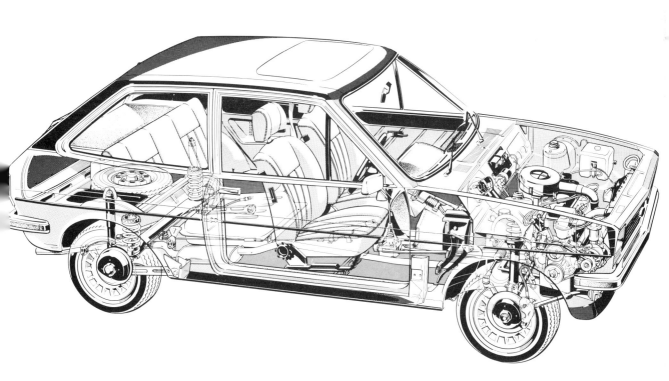

But there was another side to the company's image. After some tentative but by no means unsuccessful forays into rallying in the 1950s, Ford had begun a major onslaught on the world of motorsport in the 1960s. Highlights were four successive victories in the prestigious Le Mans 24-hour race from 1966 to 1969, and Graham Hill's Formula 1 World Championship in 1968, the first of no less than twelve to be won with the Ford-inspired Cosworth DFV series of engines. In rallying, the Cortina laid the foundations and then the Mk1 and Mk2 Escorts built up a tremendous record of success at national and international level, netting the first World Championship, both for drivers and makes, with Björn Waldegaard in 1979. Perhaps even more important, in terms of how the enthusiast saw the company, was that Ford cars and engines made their mark in almost every category from the grass-roots of club motorsport upwards.

Models like the Cortina GT, first seen in 1963, and its successors in the Escort range, carried the sporting influence through into the showroom, providing affordable performance cars within the reach of many buyers. The cumulative effect was that the Ford marque had a central position in the world of the motoring enthusiast. Traditional builders of sports cars like MG and Austin-Healey were effectively banished to the sidelines in the eyes of many people. So naturally when the Fiesta appeared, the newest new Ford for a long time, expectations ran high that there would be something in the range for the keen driver.

The small, high-performance front-wheel-drive car was not without precedent. The Mini, in its Cooper and Cooper S guises, had been *the* fun car and competition machine to a generation of enthusiasts and lingered in the affections of many. No single car among the 'superminis' had quite the same reputation but several had strong followings in their own countries. If the Fiesta was Ford's Mini, when would we see their Mini-Cooper?

It didn't look very promising at first. With an engine of only 957 or 1,117cc and skinny little tyres, the Fiesta was certainly no road burner by mid-1970s standards. But bit by bit the picture began to improve. A year after the initial launch came a 1,298cc engine, optional in Ghia and S

versions of the car. A compound dual-choke Weber carburettor helped it to a top speed of around 95mph. One spin-off from Ford's motorsport programme had been a collection of wider wheels and wheelarch extensions providing the competition-car look and marketed through the dealerships under the brand names RS and 'Series X'. A kit made available for the Fiesta provided black wheelarch spats, a matching front bib spoiler, a tailgate-mounted spoiler at the rear and alloy wheels in the four-spoke style developed by Advanced Vehicle Operations (AVO), the Ford special production unit based at Aveley in Essex.

Then, in early 1981, Ford announced a limited-edition Fiesta Supersport which had both the 1300 engine and the wider wheels, arches and spoilers. Other external details included overriders, spot-lamps and a colour-keyed grille. But the most noticeable feature of the appearance was the use of cleverly shaded decals applied to the body sides to create the illusion that the car narrowed amidships and was fitted with flared wings in the manner of the Capri X-Pack, not just the arch extensions. The interior of the Supersport combined the best of Ghia and S features, including a rev-counter on the facia. Fewer than 3,000 Supersports were produced and the model quickly became much sought-after. What insiders knew and astute Ford-watchers guessed was that the Supersport was a marketing toe-in-the-water to gauge reaction to the forthcoming XR2, the real performance Fiesta.

The Supersport had many of the features of the XR2 but not all: the principal divergence was in the engine. That was where the fact that the Fiesta had been conceived as a 'world car' became significant. When the decision had been taken to include a 'Federal' version in the Fiesta's development, for sale in the USA, it had been clear that a larger-capacity power unit would be required to meet American emission-control regulations, as well as to pull the additional weight of items like the mandatory extended '5mph' bumpers, while continuing to provide adequate performance. Consequently, though the basic European Fiesta had an engine scaled down from the Kent-series crossflow pushrod OHV unit, the US-spec car retained the full 1,598cc capacity, with the cylinder

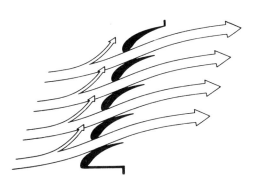

Distribution of air at low speed

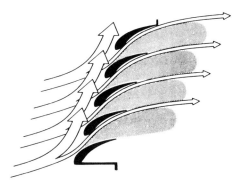

Distribution of air at high speed

Air cushion

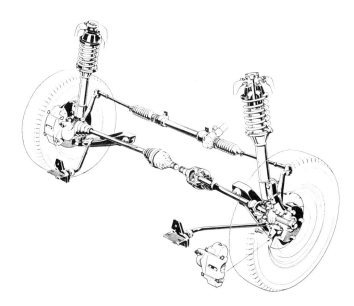

Above: The front grille with aerofoil-section slats was a neat touch: the idea was that the air-cushion effect at speed deflected air over rather than through the grille to reduce aerodynamic drag.

Left: Fiesta front suspension had MacPherson struts located at the bottom by transverse arms and radius rods. Rack-and-pinion steering and disc brakes completed the neat and simple front-end running gear.

Below: At the rear, a light dead-beam axle was located by trailing arms and a Panhard rod. Braking torque was absorbed through the damper struts.

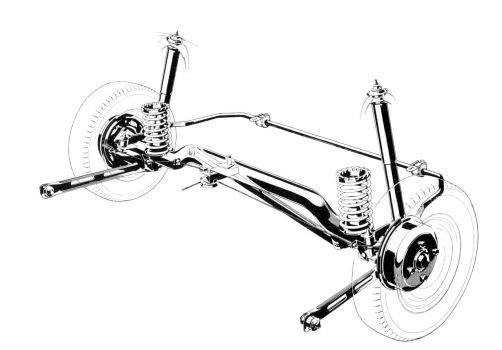

Above: Alloy wheels unique to the model and a new style of bodyside decal distinguished the XR2 from earlier sporty Fiestas. Circular headlamps were new for Europe, too (the US-market version had them) and necessitated a new location for the turn indicators in the front bumper. — Below: The transmission layout of the XR2 shared with the 1,300cc version an extra Hooke joint and steady bearing for the right-hand drive-shaft.

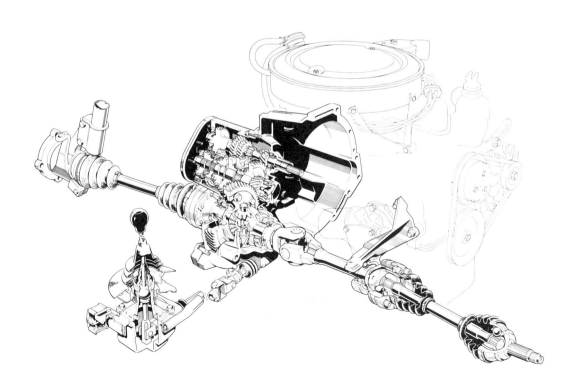

block of the formerly longitudinally-mounted engine modified where necessary for its new transverse location. So the essential bits for a 1600 Fiesta were already on the shelf.

The Ford competitions department in Britain were not slow to see the potential and they carried out considerable development work on the Fiesta. A Ford-backed one-make racing series, which later became the Ford Motor Credit Fiesta Championship, was promoted to swing attention away from the ageing rear-drive Escort and towards the new model, and, to give it the necessary zip and spectacle, the 1600 engine was admitted from 1980 — so it was raced for two seasons before it would reach the showroom. The components required, including the all-important 'Federal block' were made available through the well established competition parts operation. The specialist motoring press ran articles detailing the conversion. No doubt a good many 1600 Fiestas were created this way, and equally certainly some of them ended up on the road as well as in various forms of competition.

So when the definitive Fiesta XR2 arrived in late 1981, it was already a well proven formula. By this time, Ford had launched the second of their new-generation, transverse-engined, front-wheel-drive cars, the Mk3 Escort, and had introduced the 'XR' designation to Europe with the sporty version in that range, the XR3 of 1980. ('XR' had been used in the USA way back in the 1960s.) The new Escort shared many engineering features with the Fiesta, and its arrival meant that there were even more bits in the production parts bin to 'pick and mix' for new models.

The first-generation XR2

From the basic Fiesta, the XR2 inherited the neatly styled three-door hatchback bodyshell, conventional enough in its construction from steel pressings, but with much attention paid to avoiding unnecessary weight and complexity and to reducing the opportunities for corrosion. Despite the fairly boxy shape, low aerodynamic drag was a consideration, and some thoughtful details like the aerofoil-section slats in the front grille were incorporated to this end. Front suspension was by MacPherson struts and coil springs, with rack-and-pinion steering, and negative scrub radius geometry to help maintain straight-line stability in difficult conditions. Making the ball joint detachable from the strut was one of the details aimed at keeping service costs low. Transverse arms and simple radius rods located the bottom of the strut, and an anti-roll bar was not deemed a necessary addition for the XR2, though its suspension geometry was changed from that of ordinary Fiestas by increasing the castor angle, lowering the radius rod mountings to give more anti-dive effect under braking, and lowering the ride height. At the rear, the Fiesta had a simple dead beam axle located by trailing links and a Panhard rod, with braking torque cleverly fed into the telescopic dampers by locating pins on the axle. The rear anti-roll bar of the S version was retained for the XR2 and spring rates too were as on the S, but there were new damper settings.

The tiny front disc brakes of the basic car were replaced for the XR2 by the larger, ventilated discs from the 1.6 Escort (retained, incidentally, for the XR3 as well) but the Fiesta's rear drums were unchanged, though they had bigger slave cylinders inside them. The servo was as for the Escort. Diagonally split dual-circuit hydraulics with a tandem master cylinder were standard. The basic design was for left-hand drive, so right-hand-drive cars had to have a transverse shaft linkage from the pedal to the servo and master cylinder, and this could sometimes give rise to a sloppy pedal under very hard usage.

The alloy wheels, of 13in diameter and 6in width, were a new design for the XR2 in a 12-hole style like those used on the Capri 2.8i. The standard tyre size was 185/60HR, generous for a relatively light car and contributing to its purposeful appearance as well as its good roadholding. Wheelarch extensions to cover those tyres were in black plastic, much like those of the Supersport, as were the front and rear spoilers. But circular headlamps, for the first time on a European Fiesta, combined with the new wheels and a new style of

Left: Underbonnet view of the XR2, with the air cleaner clearly indicating the capacity of the engine. The burglar-alarm siren is a non-standard addition to this particular car.

Below: Inside the XR2 there were grey velour seats which provided adequate lateral support, a two-spoke steering wheel and a centre console. The instrument cluster with rev counter was as previous top-of-the-range versions.

shaded body-side decal treatment, made the new car clearly distinguishable from any earlier version. Twin spotlamps mounted in front of the grille just inboard of the headlamps were standard fittings.

The 1,598cc power unit had the cast-iron five-bearing block of the Federal Fiesta, and the Cortina/Escort/Capri origins of the engine design meant that the well proven GT-specification camshaft and cylinder head could be adopted more or less unchanged. A Weber 32/34 DFT carburettor, like that on the XR3, was fitted on a new inlet manifold. The engine produced a little less power than had the same basic design in earlier rear-drive models, perhaps because lack of space dictated a less favourable shape for the new exhaust manifold, but 84bhp was plenty for the purpose.

The Fiesta had the gearbox on the end of the engine with the final drive just behind, as is now virtually the norm for transverse layouts, avoiding the complexity and noise of the transfer gears made necessary by the gearbox-in-the-sump arrangement of the Mini. In the case of the XR2, the transaxle was a four-speed unit borrowed straight from the 1.6 Escort (with a slightly higher final-drive ratio than in the XR3). The overall ratio gave 18.45mph per 1,000rpm in top gear, so 70mph equated to about 3,800rpm.

Inside the XR2 there were sports seats in a grey velour material, and a two-spoke steering wheel. The standard Fiesta binnacle housed an instrument panel with 140mph speedometer and rev-counter flanking a row of warning lights and a dual temperature and fuel gauge. Details included a digital clock on the screen rail above the rear-view mirror. A Ford push-button radio was standard, with a choice of stereo radio/cassette players among the optional extras. The principal extra was the grandly styled 'climate control pack' comprising a sunroof which would flip up or could be lifted out, opening quarter-lights on the doors and a driver's side mirror with internal joystick adjustment. Black paint cost extra, as did a metallic finish.

The XR2 was announced in September 1981, went into production in October and was on sale in Britain before the end of the year. It soon began to make friends. It was nippy and responsive, with plenty of useful torque in the mid-range, and the handling won universal praise. Nobody complained about the ride, either, which was good enough for a small car of the period, if not brilliant in absolute terms. Above all, everyone found it fun to drive. On cross-country journeys through the lanes and secondary roads, it could cheerfully keep up with much more costly and powerful machinery. A not infrequent comment was that the ready and willing way the engine delivered the power and the precise and predictable handling made it a pleasanter car than the more expensive and more complicated XR3. Average performance figures put the top speed at around the 105mph mark, with 0-60mph acceleration in just under 9.5 seconds. Road test mpg figures were in the high 20s which meant that many owners would get 30mpg or more.

It all added up to a recipe which the public found very acceptable, and sales were brisk. It wasn't just Ford's customers who liked it either: it is reported that Sam Toy, Chairman of Ford of Britain at the time, would eschew his chauffeur-driven Granada when possible for the fun of driving an XR2. The model was to run until early 1984, by which time UK sales would have amounted to 20,000, when changes in the mainstream Fiesta range on which it depended would bring about a major revision.

Above: XR2 in action. The stick-on sill embellishments were particularly prominent on light-coloured examples and unfortunately did tend to emphasise any discrepancy in panel fit.
Below: At the rear, the XR2 had identification by a decal which appeared much less prominent than this on red-painted cars, and a spoiler mounted below the tailgate window.

Fiesta Ghia for 1984. New front wings, bonnet, bumpers and lamps effected an amazingly complete transformation in the car's appearance and successfully updated it for another five years' production.

XR2 Mk2. Owner Paul Cooper took first place in class with this car in the XR Owners Club National Day concours, September 1990. (Paul Cooper photo)

More than a face-lift: the second XR2

When the XR2 appeared, the basic Fiesta had already been around for five years. A year or two on from that, it was beginning to look rather dated in comparison with the opposition. Ford had anticipated the problem, of course: on the one hand they were not yet ready to make the very large investment needed to develop a completely new model, but on the other hand mere cosmetics, simply fiddling about with badges, grilles and lamps, were unlikely to be enough in the context of an increasingly competitive and demanding market-place. So the existing design was examined in detail and improved where necessary in a thorough reworking, but with most of the basic engineering unchanged. When the process was complete, there were modifications in three principal areas.

Two of those areas of change were immediately apparent when the first of the new Fiestas began to reach the showrooms in late 1983. Although the three-door bodyshell was not significantly altered aft of the windscreen, a restyled front end with a more curving bonnet line and wings to match managed to give the whole car a more rounded look, in keeping with the contemporary trend away from angular styles. Deeper, more rounded bumpers contributed to the effect, and the tail lamps were remodelled to suit. To go with the new exterior, the interior was transformed with a new facia layout, revised minor controls and a new heating and ventilation system, as well as upgraded seating for the cheaper versions. Together, the inside and outside revisions went a long way towards making it seem like an altogether new car. It was a masterful exercise which successfully updated the Fiesta's image and gave it the required new lease of life.

The third change was less evident but more fundamental. Under the bonnet, the front chassis rails incorporated in the inner wings had been reshaped to allow the fitting of the new CVH engine, first seen in the Mk3 Escort, and its attendant five-speed gearbox. This alternative power unit was not immediately made available: it first appeared in the 1.3 Fiesta Ghia in mid-1984. Enthusiasts had to wait until the autumn, about a year after the first revised Fiestas had been seen, before they could buy the new version of the XR2, though there were earlier road tests in the magazines to whet their appetites.

First impressions were favourable: the restyled nose suited the XR2 well. In its new form, the car retained black plastic wheelarch extensions but they were now joined by side skirts running along the sills. The area beneath the front bumper was now all black, so that bumper and spoiler were more closely visually linked. At the back, the horizontal spoiler beneath the window of the older model had given way to a new design which framed the top and sides of the hatch. As before, black paint was used to emphasise the side window shape on lighter coloured cars, and there were now twin coachlines along the body, but the shaded decals had no place in the new style. The circular headlamps which had previously set XR2s apart from lesser Fiestas had gone, the standard rectangular shape suiting the new bonnet and wing line better, but twin spotlamps were still standard fittings. The overall effect was more elegant and better integrated than previously, so that the 'Mk2' XR2 looked more like a car in its own right and less like a conversion.

The new interior was an improvement too, more luxurious and with less of a 'small-car' feel to it.

Above: The XR2 adopted the new shape very neatly, with sill extensions added between the wheelarch spats. Twin spotlamps remained but the headlamps were now as for other Fiestas.

Below: Rearward appearance of the new car was rendered distinctive by a new spoiler framing the upper part of the tailgate. This example has the now standard steel wheels with drilled-disc trims.

The new facia with its fingertip switches and lidded glove box was as on other top-specification revised Fiestas but the speedometer and rev counter were special to the XR2, the former reading to 140mph, the latter with a warning line from 5,800rpm and a red line at 6,500rpm. Details like the door oddment bins and the split folding rear seat added to the practicality of the car. Front seats and sound insulation were both improved, making for less tiring long-distance motoring. The new plastic steering wheel had large circular holes in its two broad spokes, a styling flourish not universally appreciated. As before, a tilt or lift-out sunroof was an extra but a remote-control driver's door mirror and rear fog lights came as standard.

The suspension, steering and brakes of the XR2 were basically much as before, with only detail modifications. At the front, run-of-the-mill Fiestas now had the lower radius-rod mountings originally developed for the XR2, so in that respect there was less deviation from standard than before. The XR2's ride height remained lower, though, and it had its own spring rates and damper settings. There were also changes to the castor and camber angles, aimed at reducing the sometimes twitchy behaviour of the old XR2 in difficult conditions but without devaluing the roadholding. All this was the result of a lot of work which Ford's Special Vehicle Engineering unit at Dunton in Essex had put into refining the car's ride and handling. Partly, it was a response to the demands of an increasingly sophisticated market and competition from newer designs, partly it was because the engineers themselves had evolved improved techniques for fine-tuning suspension systems. What is fascinating to the layman is that castor and camber changes of well under half a degree were reckoned to be significant.

The one clearly visible change in the running gear was that the alloy wheels, previously standard, were now an extra-cost option. The newly standard steel wheels, still the same 6J x 15in size, were fitted with reinforced plastic trim discs pierced by a single row of small holes and looking at a quick

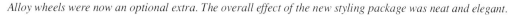

Alloy wheels were now an optional extra. The overall effect of the new styling package was neat and elegant.

Inside, the facia and trim of the new-series Fiesta created a more luxurious feel. Switches were now more easily reached, and the heating and ventilation system was new. The steering wheel was an XR2 signature.

The biggest change in the XR2's technical specification was the adoption of the CVH engine, in XR3 tune. To the right in this picture is the plastic cover over the camshaft drive belt.

glance just like another design in alloy. New drive-shafts to the front wheels, now of unequal length like those of most other Fiestas, in place of the equal-length arrangement of the first XR2, had uprated universal joints borrowed from the newly introduced diesel-engined version. Elsewhere, a 40-litre fuel tank had been insinuated into the space previously occupied by a 34-litre one. A new exhaust system had been the principal reason for the delay in getting the revised XR2 onto the market for its planned debut in June 1984: at a late stage, the rear silencer had been found to have too small a margin of durability in prolonged high-speed motoring and a revised component containing a ceramic absorption material had to be tested and substituted.

But it was the reason for fitting a new exhaust system in the first place, of course, which was the big news with the second-generation XR2. The most important change from the 'Mk1' specification was the 1,596cc single-overhead-camshaft CVH engine which replaced the venerable Kent-series unit. The engine, which had first been seen publicly in the Mk3 Escort in 1980, was an all-new design emanating from a programme of co-operation between Ford's technical staff in several European centres and the USA, a formidable combination of engineering talent reinforced by extensive use of computer analysis. It was produced in a new, highly automated plant at Bridgend in South Wales. The cylinder block and the sturdy five-bearing crankshaft were both of cast-iron, conventional enough but carefully calculated to provide adequate strength and noise suppression within tight cost limits.

The aluminium alloy cylinder head was the most original part of the design and gave the engine its designation, CVH for 'Compound Valve-angle Hemispherical chamber'. Social and legislative pressure on car manufacturers to produce more economical and less polluting engines had led to renewed research into the combustion process and its control, and the CVH head was a result of Ford's work in that field. It aimed to achieve the efficiency

Rivals: The car which the motoring press constantly set up as the standard for comparison in the 'hot hatchback' stakes was the Peugeot 205GTI. The XR2 gave it a good run for its money.

of the classic hemispherical combustion chamber without the cost and complexity of twin camshafts. Good breathing without the elaboration of more than two valves per cylinder was also a requirement. Two rows of valves at an included angle of 45 degrees were operated by rockers from a single central camshaft. The really unusual detail was that, to permit optimum valve and port sizes and to encourage the kind of circular gas-flow conducive to complete combustion, the valves were also angled at 7 degrees along the axis of the engine. That was made geometrically possible by pivoting the rockers on individual ball studs rather than a common shaft. Combining with the head to produce the complex combustion chamber shape and high compression ratios Ford wanted were pistons with ridged and bevelled crowns.

In the limited space available between the valves, smaller than usual sparking plugs, with a 14mm thread and 16mm or 5/8in AF hexagon, were installed at an angle. Hydraulic tappets completed a head design of far greater sophistication than the cast-iron pushrod OHV unit it superseded, and provided a maintenance-free top end with no need for valve clearance adjustment. The camshaft was driven by a toothed belt which also turned the water pump. Since the oil pump was mounted around the 'front' end of the crankshaft and the fuel pump and distributor were driven by the camshaft, the engine needed no jackshaft or other auxiliary drive beyond a simple V-belt to the alternator.

As fitted to the XR2, the engine was in exactly the same state of tune as had been used in the XR3, that model in turn having been replaced by the fuel-injected XR3i to maintain the proper distance between Fiesta and Escort high-performance derivatives. It had its own camshaft but was otherwise internally as for any 1.6 Escort, neither the 9.5:1 compression ratio nor the valve sizes needing amendment. Fed by a compound twin-choke downdraught Weber 32/34 DFT carburettor (the same type that had served on the earlier OHV engine, suitably re-jetted), it developed 96bhp at 6,000rpm and 98lb/ft of torque at 4,000rpm. Comparison with the output of the previous unit, 84bhp at 5,500rpm and 91lb/ft at 2,800rpm, hints at the different character of the newer engine, more powerful at higher revs by a significant margin but with proportionally less low-down lugging ability.

Helping to make use of that increased and redistributed spread of power was the five-speed gearbox. It had the standard Escort ratios, with the final drive of the ordinary 1.6 saloon rather than the lower-geared XR3 fitment, giving it a long-legged 22.9mph per 1,000rpm top gear, so 70mph meant just over 3,000rpm. The weight of the new model was up on the old, but only by about 5%, so a definite increase in performance was to be expected.

Road-test figures confirmed that expectation, with top speeds of around 110mph and 0-60mph acceleration in just over 9 seconds. The somewhat academic top speed, incidentally, was achieved in *fourth* gear, with slightly less possible in fifth, emphasising that the latter was a relaxed cruising ratio. Fuel consumption averaged around 33 or 34mpg, indicating greater overall efficiency than the 'Mk1' version. Better trim and higher gearing made the car a more pleasant long-distance machine than before, though it was still not really at its best as a motorway cruiser — sheer lack of size, if nothing else, made it susceptible to crosswind buffeting. Nimbleness, agility and a perky, fun-to-drive character were still its strong suits. If the engine needed to be revved more than before to pull the car out of corners, a precise gearchange made that no chore and the bonus of improved acceleration compensated. Many found the steering and handling sharper and more precise than before, and it took an unsympathetic driver to expose the twitchy limits. More recent and sophisticated designs like the Peugeot 205GTI, which received great attention in the motoring press, certainly gave the XR2 some stiff competition, but when the purchase price and low running costs of the Ford were taken into consideration it acquitted itself very well. That fun-per-pound-Sterling factor continued to win many admirers. Through nearly five years of production, the revised XR2 continued to sell well, accounting for at least one in ten of all UK Fiesta sales, until the basic model was displaced by a new car in early 1989.

Third generation: the XR2i

The first Fiesta, in its original and revised forms, was very successful for Ford: it stayed in production for 12 years and almost five million examples, across the range, were built. But it couldn't go on for ever, and even before the face-lifted version had been launched in 1983, work on a replacement had begun. Because the market which awaited the new car had changed appreciably from the one into which Ford's first venture in the 'supermini' category had been launched back in the mid-1970s, a significantly different design would be called for. Ford referred to the 'superminis' as 'B-Class' cars, 'A-Class' being the shrinking category for smaller vehicles like the Fiat 126. 'B-Class' constituted a much larger proportion of European sales than before and there were more contenders in the field, both factors which demanded higher standards and more choice for the buyer if the new Ford were to be competitive. More internal space and the possibility of a five-door option were key requirements identified by Ford analysts. The pressure was still on for improvements in economy and efficiency and reductions in emissions. Further cuts in servicing costs would be welcome, and there were new production techniques to be considered. It all added up to pretty much of a 'clean-sheet' start again, although this time, of course, there would be many lessons learnt already with the Fiesta to be applied. The power units would be carried over into the new model, albeit comprehensively revised. And, because of the success of the XR2, which had constituted up to a quarter of all Fiestas sold at some periods later in the run, an XR version would be developed in the range from the beginning, not tacked on later.

The importance Ford attached to making a success of the new Fiesta is reflected in the comprehensive research and careful development which went into the project. Many aspects of the design were referred back to the buying public, through surveys, styling 'clinics' at which mock-ups were shown alongside potential competitors, and, later in the programme, test-driving sessions at which unidentified prototypes were available to be driven, not just looked at. In this way, the engineers and designers were constantly kept in touch with what the people who might eventually buy the car actually wanted.

Along with all the technical development required, it took up a great deal of time and gave rise to countless internal meetings. The basic concept of the car was fixed more than six years before the launch. By that time, some possibilities, like the 'tall' look introduced by the Fiat Uno and Honda City, had already been considered and eliminated. Complete prototypes, very close in detail to the finished article and containing a very high proportion of production-standard components, were running two years ahead of the public debut. So the car — a whole range of cars, really, with twice as many variants as in the old style — which was launched in February 1989 and reached the showrooms a couple of months later was one of the most thoroughly tried and tested new models ever.

The new Fiesta emerged as a neatly styled, smart, up-to-date three or five-door hatchback which was slightly larger and much roomier than the car it replaced. The wheelbase was increased by 6in (making it nearly two inches longer than that of the Mk3 Escort, but then that model too was due for replacement soon) and the track went up by 1.8in. But a feature of the new shape was its 'wheels-at-the-corners' stance, and the overall length and

Left: The all-new Fiesta for 1989 was a smooth design, slightly larger all round than its predecessor, and with a pronounced wheel-at-each-corner stance. This Popular Plus is in the commercially important five-door form: the higher-performance derivatives would all adopt the three-door shell.

Left: The Fiesta S had a carburettor-fed 1.6-litre engine and was fitted with a rear tailgate-top spoiler. In many ways, its speci-fication echoed that of the old XR2, but it was less overtly sporty.

Right: Standard-equipment twin spot-lamps were another XR2 echo in the presentation of the new Fiesta 1.6S.

Above: Wide wheels and a comprehensive body kit, with spot and fog lamps in the front air-dam, gave the XR2i an altogether more aggressive and purposeful look than the ordinary new-generation Fiestas. Wheelarch and sill extensions and bumpers were now colour-matched to the paintwork, though the door mirrors remained black.

Below: A deeper and wider rear skirt, with a prominent cut-out for the squared-up exhaust tailpipe, distinguished the rear view of the XR2i from that of the 1.6S with which it shared the roof-level spoiler.

This page: External details of the XR2i included new alloy wheels with a tangential six-spoke pattern, spoiler-mounted auxiliary lamps at the front, decal badging in the style established with earlier XRs, and rear lamp units which neatly incorporated fog and reversing lights.

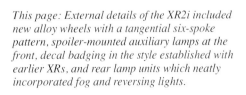

width were increased by smaller amounts than the chassis dimensions, just 3.7in and 0.8in respectively. There was more glass area, 10% more, and the sloping bonnet and windscreen, as well as much careful detailing, helped make the car 15% more aerodynamically efficient — reducing wind noise and keeping the windows clean were important reasons for that improvement, as well as straightforward drag reduction. The new car's headroom, legroom and shoulder room were claimed to be the best in its class and luggage space was up by no less than 45% on the old Fiesta. And, despite the fact that strength and durability were given higher priority than lightness, computer-aided design had kept the increase in unladen weight down to 50 or 60lb for comparable models.

So much for the basic car, obviously a very competent piece of mainstream engineering: but what of the higher performance version or versions to delight the enthusiast? As launched, the range included an S version fitted with a 1.6-litre engine much like that of the old XR2 but detuned to produce 90bhp at 5,800rpm. The peak torque figure remained the same, 98lb/ft at 4,000rpm, but a flatter torque curve and better fuel consumption were claimed. The performance figures were very close to those of the XR2. It had slightly fatter tyres than the 'cooking' models, 165/65SR13 on 5in wide rims, and its cockpit equipment included a rev counter. Otherwise, it was to be distinguished from the other Fiestas with L trim only by special wheel trims, two spotlamps at the front and a small spoiler on the top edge of the tailgate. As a sporty but unpretentious extension of the Fiesta range it had its place and was welcome enough, but the real XR was still to come, held back while initial production was concentrated on the models expected to sell in the largest numbers.

When it arrived, in the second half of 1989, the XR2i had a much more clearly defined identity. Wheelarch and sill extensions and new, deep-skirted front and rear bumper sections, ornamented with inset blue piping, transformed the Fiesta's neat but somewhat bland styling, giving it a new purposeful and powerful look. Wheels with 5.5in-wide rims, steel as standard but with a new design in alloy optional, carried 185/60HR13 tyres to fill

out the widened arches. Four auxiliary lamps were incorporated in the front air-dam. The rear upper spoiler, like that of the 1.6S, was black, but the other body additions were colour-keyed to match the paintwork, further distancing the car from the ordinary Fiestas with their grey-black bumpers and striking a more fashion-conscious and elegant styling note than the black add-ons of the old XR2.

Inside, the XR2i was less different from other top-range Fiestas, since they were already well fitted out, but the seats provided a little more side support, and additional equipment included central locking, electric window lifts, a remote tailgate release and a centre console. The tilt or lift-out sunroof now came as standard. Better sound insulation was included too. The fat two-spoke steering wheel was from the 1.6S. Blue lines on the door panels, carpets and gear-lever top were special to the XR2i and echoed the external trim.

Under the skin, the XR2i had been developed along with the rest of the range, not as a separate SVE project, and it shared many components with other models. Front suspension for all the new Fiestas retained the familiar MacPherson-strut principle but in heavily revised form. In place of the transverse link and radius rod there was now an L-shaped lower arm pivoting on two bonded rubber bushes which were bolted in a vertical rather than the more usual horizontal position. The front bush on each side was spherical to provide accurate location, while the rear one was designed to deform under load to give a measure of compliance for straight-line stability over bumps. An anti-roll bar was fitted to the XR2i and a less stiff one to the 1.6S. All models had much revised geometry compared with the old Fiesta, with a lower front roll centre in the interests of stability. A new rack and less castor angle had made the steering lighter, but at the expense of lower gearing, now 4.2 turns lock-to-lock.

At the rear, the dead beam axle of the previous model had gone, to be replaced by a semi-independent twisting beam layout. Trailing arms were linked by a torsion beam which both controlled their alignment and acted as an anti-roll bar. It was a neat and effective design, the principle having first been seen on the VW Golf and, in

Above: Facia of the XR2i, with good provision for fresh-air ventilation, and distinctive quadrant instruments shaped to be visible through the steering wheel.
Below: The interior had well bolstered seats in a distinctive check fabric, and less of a 'small-car' driving position than the earlier model.

Above: Cutaway drawing of the XR2i reveals the principal features of the design including the revised CVH engine and the new-generation Fiesta shell, in two-door form, with added wheelarch spats, sill extensions and spoilers.

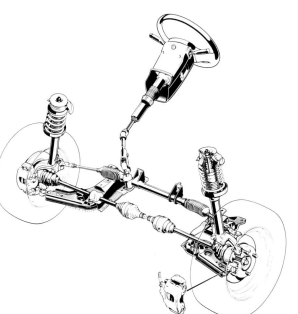

Left: The front suspension of the new Fiesta remained faithful to the MacPherson strut principle, but with L-shaped lower wishbones instead of the earlier transverse arms. Inboard mountings for the wishbones incorporated rubber bushes carefully calculated to provide both precise location and a measure of controlled compliance.

Below: Although illustrated here on a four-door car, the electro-mechanical anti-lock braking system was an option on the XR2i as well as other Fiestas. Sensors belt-driven from the inboard driveshaft joints modulated hydraulic pressure in the event of wheel locking. Also evident in this drawing is the neat and compact semi-independent rear suspension design.

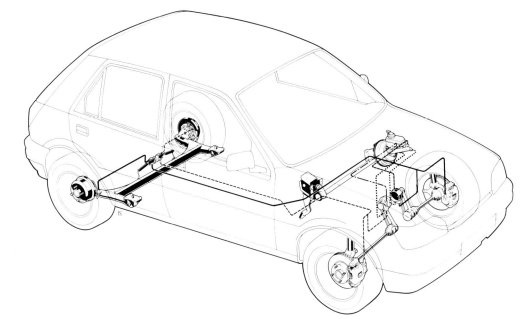

conjunction with the forward location of the fuel tank, under the rear seat pan, it allowed for a much lower rear floor than before, contributing to that increased luggage space. The XR2i had its own spring rates and damper settings, front and rear.

Disc front and drum rear brakes were actuated by a diagonally-split dual hydraulic circuit, as before. The XR2i and 1.6S shared bigger, ventilated front discs which had a new, single-piston caliper design, and the rear drums were enlarged for the faster models this time, to 8in diameter. But the major innovation on the braking front was the availability of the Lucas-Girling mechanical antilock system (SCS, for 'Stop Control System') as an option at an extra cost of £400. Sensors driven from the drive-shafts detected locking at either front wheel and in response relieved hydraulic pressure both to that brake and to the diagonally opposite rear brake. First seen on the Escort in 1986, the system was a commendable attempt to provide a lower-priced alternative to the complex ABS fitted to Sierra Cosworths, BMWs, Audis and the like, but it met with a mixed reaction, some hard drivers objecting to the way it interfered with pedal response yet did not entirely eliminate the possibility of wheel-locking.

Under the bonnet of the XR2i was the reason for the addition of that little 'i' to the designation, a fuel-injected version of the 1,596cc CVH engine. Rather than simply transplanting the power unit from the Escort XR3i, Ford had taken the opportunity to revise and improve it. They called the new unit EFI for 'Electronic Fuel Injection': the once ubiquitous Bosch K-Jetronic mechanical fuel-injection was replaced by a new arrangement using Weber injectors. Also new was a transistorised direct ignition system in which a flywheel sensor and two dual-output coils replaced the conventional coil and distributor. Both fuel injection and ignition were under the control of Ford's own EEC IV electronic engine management unit. There were also revisions to the camshaft and the manifolds.

The net effect was a power output of 110bhp at 6,000rpm, compared with 105bhp for the XR3i and 96bhp for the carburettor-fed XR2. Peak torque was 102lb/ft, the same as for the earlier injection engine, but developed much lower down the rev range, at 2,800rpm instead of 4,800, indicating a big step forward in usable flexibility. The familiar five-speed transaxle had the gearchange linkage redesigned to improve its action and was fitted with a lower final-drive ratio than before to give overall

The new EFI version of the 1.6-litre CVH engine had integrated electronic control for the fuel injection and distributor-less ignition system. Other aspects of the unit were basically as before but revised in detail.

Side view of a dark-coloured XR2i emphasises the longer and lower look of the new shape. The sunshine roof was part of the standard equipment.

gearing of 20.3mph per 1,000rpm in fifth. The new, more fully equipped car was something like 100lb heavier than the old XR2, but more aerodynamic as well as more powerful. Ford promised a top speed of 119mph, 0-60mph acceleration in 9 seconds and (unleaded) petrol consumption of 30mpg or better.

Those performance claims turned out to be about right when the XR2i was independently tested. Drivers liked the cabin, roomier than the old model and feeling even more so because of the large glass area and light-coloured trim. The suspension, significantly stiffer than that of the ordinary new Fiestas, delivered good roadholding and open-road ride, though perhaps a bit harsh at low speeds in town. Good low and middle-range torque made the car pleasant to drive and obviated the need to venture often into the upper rev range, where the engine was criticised for harshness and resonance. The build quality and finish, particularly inside, were reckoned to be above average for a mass-produced vehicle, though there were some reservations about the fit of the external 'body-kit'. The overall impression was of a well equipped and good-looking car. Even at about £1,200 more than the outgoing XR2, it seemed like fairly good value and likely to prove popular.

The one drawback highlighted by most testers was the low-geared steering which deprived the

Above: The Fiesta RS Turbo had the external features of the XR2i with the addition of bonnet vents, a larger front air-intake and its own distinctive 14in-diameter three-spoke wheels. — Below: Evident in this threequarter view of the RS Turbo are the lowered rear ride-height and body-coloured spoiler. A much larger rear spoiler was tried to good effect during development but not adopted for production.

XR2i of the really sharp and responsive handling expected of a contender in the 'hot hatchback' class. An awful lot of owners were no doubt going to be perfectly happy with it, but some journalists were moved to use phrases like 'dull-witted' when they compared the car with, for example, the Peugeot 205GTI. Part of the problem was that the increase in price, size and power output over the old model had subtly changed the hot Fiesta's position in relation to the not always easy to define categories into which such cars were perceived to fit. It was now seen to be in head-on competition in the very keenly contested 'GTI' group, rather than leading a kind of junior league.

Insofar as Ford needed to respond to the criticism, with business brisk in the showrooms, their answer was, in effect, 'wait and see': the *really* sporting Fiesta, they hinted, was still to come. That model was the Fiesta RS Turbo and it appeared in June 1990: it was planned to have only a limited production span, perhaps 20,000 cars in two years. Ford made it clear that they regarded the cars as two very distinct models, and they did not expect many buyers to swop from one to the other. They estimated that the RS Turbo would account for 2% of all Fiesta sales, compared with 14% for the XR2i. Externally, the RS Turbo had the XR2i's body additions, but with a colour-matched rear spoiler and green instead of blue piping inserts. It had its own three-spoke alloy road wheels with 5.5in x 14in rims carrying 185/55VR14 tyres. It had a vented bonnet panel and a slightly enlarged front air intake, evidence of the new power unit inside. The engine combined elements of the XR2i EFI unit and that of the Escort RS Turbo, with a new, smaller turbocharger and more efficient ducting and intercooling: it produced 133bhp, with 135lb/ft available at 2,400rpm and an almost flat torque curve up to 5,000rpm.

It could have been rather confusing, two high-performance variants in the same model range. To help explain the distinction between them, Ford's publicity agents Ogilvy & Mather ran an advert likening the two cars to Madras and Vindaloo — hot and very hot. More prosaically, the difference was £1,100 at early 1991 prices, just over 10% on top of the XR2i figure. Plus whatever it added to your insurance (group 5 for the XR2i, group 6 for the RS Turbo), plus more petrol, plus, no doubt, higher long-term maintenance costs with a turbocharged engine.

So what did you get for your extra outlay with the RS version? Well, a blistering 130mph top speed — if you could find anywhere to use it. Scorching acceleration: 0-60mph in 7.7 seconds, according to Ford, and on up to 100mph in 20 seconds or thereabouts. But of much more practical relevance were extensively modified suspension and steering. While the XR2i had been developed along with all the other new Fiestas, the RS Turbo had been referred to the wizards at Special Vehicle Engineering. Within the tight constraints of controlled costs and the prohibition of any changes to the mass-production sheet-metalwork, they had reworked the chassis, changing the damper settings all round and the rear spring rates, lowering the rear ride-height, replacing the front lower arms and ball joints to alter the geometry, adding a rear anti-roll bar and adopting the 14in wheel and tyre size already mentioned. Out went the 'slow' steering rack of the ordinary Fiesta, to be replaced by one giving a much more appropriate 3.75 turns lock-to-lock. The result was much closer to the sporting handling which the journalists had been looking for. Chassis design is always a compromise, though, and pushing the balance towards sharp, precise responses incurred a debit in terms of poorer ride quality, heavier steering and less refinement.

Then in October 1990 there was a rumour that the XR2i was to get RS Turbo-specification suspension and steering. It's still too early to say with any certainty what that would do for the car's reputation — or indeed to assess what kind of reputation the XR2i will establish for itself at all. One thing that seems clear, though, is that however good a car it may be in its own right, it really isn't a direct replacement for the XR2. Maybe that's inevitable: time doesn't stand still, the pace of progress in car design has been rapid in recent decades, and the demands of the market are ever-changing. But it does help firmly to establish the XR2 as a minor classic.

Above: The turbocharged XR2 developed by Turbo Technics was engineered to a very high standard and accepted for sale by Ford dealers. It provided a big increase in performance without spoiling tractability.

Left: Under the bonnet of the Turbo Technics XR2 can be seen the intercooler and the air feed to the standard but recalibrated carburettor.

The hot Fiesta and the tuners

From the manufacturer's point of view, car enthusiasts as a breed are hard to satisfy. Make an ordinary car and it's almost certain that somebody will improve it — or try to, anyway, try to make it go faster, accelerate more quickly, go round corners better. Take an ordinary car, improve it yourself, as Ford did with the Fiesta to produce the XR2, and market the result as an addition to the range, and a lot of customers will be very happy; but there will still be some who want more performance, better roadholding, more equipment.

The XR2, particularly after the 1984 revision, had a very well developed chassis, endowing it with handling and roadholding better than many of its rivals. But as competition in the 'hot hatchback' category grew, it began to be left behind in the horsepower race. The basic engine was not the limitation: the appearance of progressively more powerful versions in the Escort range for the XR3i, the RS1600i and the RS Turbo proved that the CVH unit could provide more bhp, even in production form. For Ford, the difficulty was a marketing one, arising from the need to keep the Fiesta and Escort in their rightful relative places in the hierarchy of models. Occasionally, though, there were ways of bending the rules.

Turbo Technics was an independent company which had built up an excellent reputation for well engineered turbocharger conversions and had plenty of experience with the CVH engine, having been turbocharging Escorts since early 1982. They had established a good working relationship with Ford, the two companies having co-operated on a number of projects including a Capri 2.8 Turbo, and Ford thought highly enough of their work to authorise the marketing of their conversions through Ford dealers. This, then, was an ideal way of getting a turbo XR2 to meet the demand for a Fiesta to rival cars like the Renault 5 Turbo without tying up Ford's own development resources and without directly undermining the hotter Escorts.

The installation which Turbo Technics developed used a Garrett AiResearch water-cooled turbocharger supplying air through an intercooler to the standard XR2 carburettor, suitably modified and fed by a new high-pressure electric fuel pump. A redesigned exhaust manifold cast in high-quality iron was used, and the ignition timing curve and spark plug specification were revised. The maximum power output was boosted to 125bhp. Upgraded front suspension bushes were the only chassis modification required, an indication of how good the standard set-up was.

Ford dealers were able to offer complete cars, with a warranty extended to cover any turbo-related problems, for just under £8,600, compared with just over £7,200 for the normal XR2 at 1987 prices. Testers found a complete absence of temperamental behaviour and none of the sudden and embarrassing rush of power characteristic of some less competent turbo conversions, rating the car as easy to drive at low speeds as any ordinary Fiesta. Yet it would surge from rest to 60mph in under 8 seconds and the top speed was over 120mph. Even more significantly, the 50-70mph time of the standard XR2 was halved. All this extra performance had not unbalanced the handling and the car remained surefooted and fun to drive. (With a power-to-weight ratio comparable to that of an Audi Quattro, it was perhaps not for the inexperienced, though.) One can well imagine the success of this XR2 development playing a part in Ford's decision to add an RS Turbo to the 1989 Fiesta range.

Factory-approved conversions are only the tip of the iceberg, of course. When Ford, through their involvement in motorsport and by marketing cars like the Cortina GT, began in the 1960s to assume the role of the enthusiast's marque, the process had as one of its continuing side-effects an amazing

Left: Rear view of the Turbo Technics Q-car: only a discreet decal beneath the Ford oval gives the game away.

Below: Supporting the theory that anything is possible, given the time, patience and money, is this Fiesta van into which Steve McCall grafted an Escort RS Turbo power unit. A great many problems had to be overcome but the end result was a breathtaking fun machine.

Fiesta XR2 Fly. This special XR2 is believed to be one of only 23 ever made. It is a true fun car, with three big names behind it: Ford themselves, of course; conversion experts Crayford Auto Developments, who designed it; and the Coachworks Division of F. English Limited, who brought 60 years of coachbuilding experience to the project. The Fly was available from a choice of 16 basic Fiesta models, including the option of any of the four engine sizes and a variety of colours and trim levels. Considerable expertise is required to replace the structural rigidity lost when taking the roof off an integral steel bodyshell. (XROC photos)

Additional rear spoiler from RGA Design combines neatly with the standard item and improves the high-speed stability of the XR2.

growth and proliferation in the after-market tuning and modification industry. Those first Cortinas and Escorts must surely have been the most frequently tuned and modified cars up till that time (with the possible exception of the Mini) and the pattern has been repeated with subsequent models, the Fiesta among them. A quick glance at the pages of one of the specialist magazines which carries advertising from the manufacturers and purveyors of tuning equipment will reveal an enormous variety of ways to improve and modify Ford's little hatchback.

Some of them, of course, are applicable to the smaller-engined versions, and are in effect offering the chance to try and catch up with the factory's own high-performance derivatives. The XR2, with its larger-capacity engine, Weber carburettor, wider wheels, bigger brakes and stiffer suspension, already has all the tuner's basic first steps built-in. But there's a lot more that can be done, in all sorts of different ways to suit different tastes and needs. The sky — or, more often, the budget — is the limit.

When it was endowed with the 1,600cc Kent-series crossflow engine, the first XR2 also inherited a good deal of already proven engine tuning expertise. Most of the reputable tuning firms can offer conversions for this power unit: a free-flow exhaust system is likely to be the first step, a reworked cylinder head the next. Further work would involve a change of camshaft, uprating the carburettor and balancing the moving parts.

For some time after its introduction, the CVH engine was a lot less popular with the tuners. Perhaps in part that is because it is a more advanced design and hence less susceptible to low-cost methods. But it has now been around for long enough for the better operators in the field to have accumulated valuable experience with it. The basic steps are the same as with the earlier unit, but the percentage increases in power are likely to be less because the standard engine is better to start with. Something like 115bhp can be obtained with a stage one head and new exhaust system, with a useful increase in mid-range torque which is of far more value in most driving conditions than top-end bhp, no matter what the saloon-bar boy-racers might like to tell you. At the other end of the scale, the most radical CVH conversion involves boring and linering the cylinder block and fitting special pistons, connecting rods and crankshaft to increase the cubic capacity to just under 2 litres. Not cheap, but the result is upwards of 130bhp and a torque curve like a steam engine.

Put the XR2i, with its EFI engine, alongside an early XR2 and you realise how much automobile technology has changed in less than ten years. Electronic engine management has made the car better able to perform consistently at its optimum, reducing both the scope and the need for the simpler forms of after-market tinkering. Improvements can be made, though, by the usual techniques of gas flowing inlet and exhaust tracts and meticulous attention to the cylinder head. Beyond that, as with the Cosworth Sierra, it is possible to call on the specialist skills of the firms who are able to offer alternative microchips.

For suspension modification, as for engine tuning, there is a wide range of components available, and the specialist suppliers can select springs and dampers to adjust the handling of the Fiesta to taste. Unlike many production cars, the XR2 really doesn't need wider wheels and tyres, even with a considerably uprated engine.

There are those XR2 owners, of course, who value their cars for their originality and wouldn't want to change them at all. There are others who are keen to create their own, distinctive machine, or who revel in the idea of the small high-performance bombshell and want to explore its full potential. In between, there are those for whom a degree of mild tuning enhances the pleasure of driving the car at no great cost. It may well be, for example, that with an older car in need of an overhaul it can be very cost-effective to combine some tuning with reconditioning. The usual cautions apply, however: it's a complete waste of time and money to put new tuning bits on a worn engine. And nobody but a fool increases the performance of a car which doesn't have brakes and suspension in tip-top condition and a sound bodyshell. Remember too that modified cars often fail to command higher-than-average resale prices, so unless you are definitely going to keep your XR for some time, be prepared to lose money if you embark on expensive tuning.

There have been cars which needed a fair amount of modification to make them even acceptable to the keen driver. The XR2 and XR2i certainly aren't in that category. It's just that there are always some people whose enthusiastic response to something good is to start wanting to make it better. One special reason for doing that with a car is to be competitive in some form of motorsport.

Case Study 1

POWER ENGINEERING'S SYSTEM TWO LITRE XR2

Having already developed a 2-litre conversion for the Escort XR3i, Power Engineering found it only logical to insert one of their muscular motors into an XR2 Mk2.

Not surprisingly, the extra horsepower caused a serious imbalance in the Fiesta's suspension system. The first time that the clutch was dropped with a serious number of engine revs being indicated on the tachometer, the XR2 darted first left and then right, as the wheels struggled for traction. No way could the conversion be sanctioned without a close look at the entire suspension system underpinning the XR2.

In close collaboration with the respected suspension design team at Spax, Power developed a new set of coil springs and dampers which slotted straight into the holes vacated by the original Ford items. The car sits slightly closer to the ground than the standard version and this, when combined with a couple of front-end geometry changes, acts most effectively to control the most wayward actions of the gallon beneath the bonnet of this pint-sized powerhouse.

The amount of torque which this engine develops is quite astounding. It can pull away in high gear from as little as 1,200rpm, and by 3,000 there is around one-and-a-half times the power of a standard XR2. Overall, one feels that the engine would happily continue to deliver power by the bucketful for ever, if the valve gear would only let it.

The standard clutch assembly of the Fiesta is retained, and pedal pressure and bite are fine. The gearshift is accurate and precise as long as gearchanges are not over-hurried — otherwise baulking through the gearlever mechanism will attempt to break your wrist.

Although there is a distinct extra surge at about 2,800rpm as the carb's second venturi comes into effect, engine speed is always progressively related to the amount of pressure being applied to the throttle pedal. The middle pedal is commonly the one which gives the XR2 owner cause for concern, but Power confronted this problem with a package comprising uprated front pads and rear shoes, stainless steel flexible brake lines and racing-specification fluid. The result was a marked improvement in stopping power and a far more positive pedal action.

Power's final modification was to replace the original steering wheel with a leather-trimmed Nardi wheel. While it is true that no new wheel can really overcome the weird offset of the steering column head, the tactile pleasure of the Nardi's rim provides considerable compensation.

The only time the car showed reluctance to run smoothly was when it was cold. Its auto-choked Weber carburettor has a flat spot halfway through its range which disappears when the engine has reached its proper operating temperature. This problem has been noticed on quite a number of XR2s and is apparently curable.

Amazingly, for a converted car of this calibre, a 1,400-mile 'mixed driving' test showed fuel consumption to be still economical at 32mpg.

Perhaps the only failing of the car is its lack of a soundproofing kit: on a long drive, the noise level from under the bonnet can prove tiresome. All things considered, however, there can be few more effective ways than Powers' of improving the performance of a standard XR2. On test, it proved almost unbeatable on the open highway, yet equally at home in heavy traffic.

Case Study 2

PANIQUE FIESTA STYLING SYSTEM

Paul Newton's company, *Panique*, derives its name from a combination of his initials and *unique* — 'which I hope the kits are!' Having previously produced a package of panels for the Escort Mk2, Paul recently took the plunge into full-time self-employment as an automotive stylist with this wide-arched Fiesta body styling system.

Following a great deal of thought and a vast number of styling sketches, Paul took the basic Fiesta and began building from flexible marine plywood, moulding foam and body filler. Once shaped, the panels were finished to a high standard and moulds made from them prior to copies being sprung.

To appeal to a wider market and to ensure that wheel size, and hence tyre size, would not adversely affect the car's performance, Paul decided to go for no more than moderate additional width. The most important criterion, however, was ease of fitment. Provision for this was incorporated into the next stage — readying the moulds and finalising the kit's flanges, mountings and so forth. Typical of the care taken is the treatment of the side skirt assemblies: an inner section has been developed, in the form of a U-channel, which is attached firmly to the underside of the sill and over which the styling panel slides tightly. This ensures that both the top and bottom sections of the outer panel are supported and that the outer panel fits exactly into its intended position.

The wing extensions are bonded to the car's sheet metal using a high-bond adhesive which seals them against water ingress, after which body filler is used to blend them into the original panel. The extra two inches of front width and three inches of rear width created by the new mouldings necessitate wider wheels and tyres: to accommodate these, the original wheelarches of the car have to be cut away.

For simplicity's sake, the front and rear spoiler and bumper mouldings have been designed around the originals and use the same mounting points, making installation a straightforward bolt-on job. The front spoiler comes with a pair of Cosworth driving lamps ready to wire into the main lighting circuit. The rear under-spoiler is moulded to accommodate the original reversing lamp. The rear foglamp is left to the owner, as there are various permutations for such fitments.

The high-rise tailgate aerofoil is another bolt-on affair, the complete assembly being attached to the tailgate with four fasteners. The wing fits cars both with and without a rear wash-wipe mechanism.

Finally, the package provides a pair of Sierra RS Cosworth bonnet louvre vents. These slip easily into holes pre-cut in the bonnet and are affixed from their underside. Location of these is made easy by a template which is part of the complete installation pack. Templates for the four wheelarches showing precisely where the metal needs to be cut are also provided.

The glassfibre panels are finished in high-build primer and the kit comes with a tube of special bonding sealant, a full supply of nuts, bolts, screws and rivets, and, of course, illustrated step-by-step instructions.

Case studies 1 and 2 extracted from Performance Ford *magazine by kind permission of the editor.*

Left: Bill Blydenstein with the revised air intake system developed by his company for the Fiesta XR2i: a useful gain in power and torque is achieved at modest cost.

Below: Second stage of the Blydenstein conversion for the XR2i is the 'A Pack' cylinder head, the design of which draws on the company's long experience of modifying and refining production engines to improve power, torque and tractability.

Case Study 3

BLYDENSTEIN XR2i CONVERSION

Like all the sporty Fords before it, the XR2i was bound to attract the attention of the tuners. Its more sophisticated specification, compared with earlier models, makes their job more difficult, of course, but by no means impossible.

One of the best performance conversions for the XR2i to be put on the market comes from Blydenstein Racing Limited, a long-established and most highly thought-of name in the tuning business. Although well known over the years for working on Vauxhalls, Bill Blydenstein has recently been converting Fords in conjunction with Ford Rallye Sport Dealer, Gilbert Rice.

As modifying the engine management computer and changing chips are measures disapproved of by Ford, Blydenstein sticks to the classic tuning ploys, working on the mechanical components of the engine to enhance gas flow and improve combustion characteristics. The durability of the engine is not affected and the electronics remain unaltered.

The first step with the XR2i is to apply some subtle modifications, based on long experience, to the internal aerodynamics of the airbox and collector pipe, modified units being supplied on an exchange basis. This simple and inexpensive measure alone improves the through-flow of air sufficiently to add up to 5bhp to the power output. More important, it also gives a net increase of 4-5% in torque, resulting in a noticeably smoother and more driveable engine.

Blydenstein usually prefers to fit conversions at his Shepreth premises, so that the car can be set up on the rolling-road dynamometer. But there is very little that can be done in the case of the XR2i because the ignition and injection settings, with the exception of the idle screw, are factory set. So this kit can be supplied for do-it-yourself fitting.

Further work involves what the company calls its 'A Pack' cylinder head which has reprofiled ports and carefully modified combustion chambers giving optimum gas flow. In combination with the improved air-intake tract, this raises both torque and power by 10-12%. The result on the road is a car which feels smoother, freer-running and, above all, more willing and flexible. The need to keep stirring the gearlever to maintain momentum is much reduced and the change from fourth to fifth is no longer accompanied by that feeling that all acceleration has ceased. The engine keeps on pulling in top gear. Mid-range acceleration, the key to keeping up a respectable average on give-and-take roads, is the most noticeably enhanced quality.

There remains further scope for tuning, and the company is always happy to discuss bespoke conversions to suit individual requirements. Measures like raising the compression ratio, which requires the use of 98 octane petrol, will yield a further 2-3% torque and power increase. It would, though, bring a big jump in cost as well. While not available at present, exhaust manifold and system modifications would further enhance overall performance and efficiency.

As it stands, the Blydenstein package of airbox and cylinder head modifications constitutes a particularly successful conversion, and very good value for money.

(Ian Shaw photo)

The XR2 & XR2i in competition

As we have seen, there was a motorsport connection right at the very beginning of the XR2 story, at the point where it diverged from the Fiesta mainstream. Fiestas with 1,600cc engines for one-model saloon racing predated the launch of the road car. In the late 1970s, Ford's British competition department was entering a difficult period. The great international rallying career of the rear-wheel-drive Mk1 and Mk2 Escorts was coming to a close, though they would continue to be a mainstay of club sport for many years, and it was a hard act to follow. For a time, the Fiesta became the focus of attention: small and light, yet able to accommodate an engine as big as that of the Escort, it showed some promise as a competition machine. Within the framework of the prevailing fairly liberal Group 2 regulations, using the specification of the 'Federal' version as a homologation basis, the competition department at Boreham developed a rallying Fiesta which had the 1,600cc Kent engine, fed by twin dual-choke Weber carburettors to produce over 150bhp, and extensively modified suspension including new triangulated lower arms at the front. Bodywork modifications included widened wheelarches and a full roll-cage in the manner well established in the Escort days. At one stage, it even ran with a second, internal rear window to seal the luggage area off from the cockpit and safely contain the fuel cell and oil tank for the dry-sump lubrication system. A works team of two cars was entered in the 1979 Monte Carlo Rally, driven by Roger Clark and Ari Vatanen, the latter finishing tenth overall.

These were out-and-out competition cars, but the use of the Kent-series OHV engine does make them part of the XR2 lineage. Further development brought other power units into consideration and,

had the idea been pursued, we might have seen a 16-valve BDA-powered Fiesta 'homologation special' — prototypes were built. But the laws of physics took a hand. Beyond a certain power-to-weight ratio, there were traction and handling problems inherent in the front-wheel-drive layout, particularly on the loose road surfaces encountered in rallying, which were fundamentally insuperable. Technological progress, in areas like tyre compounds, the analysis of suspension geometry, power steering and new forms of limited-slip transmission, was some help, and has continued to edge the threshold upwards (lessons Ford learnt with the Fiesta about the use of viscous couplings to control differential slip have proved useful in more recent four-wheel-drive designs) but the fact remained that, however good it might be for a fast road car in the XR2/GTI mould, front-wheel-drive would not again produce a consistent top-level rally winner. The days of the little FWD giant-killer, Mini-Cooper S style, would not return. It might provide class-winners: but Ford's rallying effort had always been directed at overall victory — class wins often cost almost as much but were of much less certain publicity value.

The Fiesta shell continued to receive attention for a time, a rear-wheel-drive prototype being built in 1979, before work switched to the Escort Mk3-based RS1700T. The subsequent abandonment of that project and its replacement by the mid-engined, four-wheel-drive RS200, itself short-lived because of factors outside Ford's control, is another story. The Ford rally team was plunged into the doldrums from which it only really began to emerge in 1990 with the advent of the Sierra RS Cosworth 4x4 and the promise of its Escort-shaped successor.

Above: Cutaway drawing reveals some of the features of the 1,600cc Group 2 rallying Fiesta built by Ford's competition department at Boreham in 1979. Evident among other details are the revised front suspension and rear disc-brake conversion.

Below: The Fiesta to be driven by Roger Clark in the 1979 Monte Carlo Rally takes shape at Boreham. Clark subsequently drove the car in some British rallies but without success. Traction and handling problems were never satisfactorily resolved and the project proved short-lived.

Ari Vatanen on his way to tenth overall in the 1979 Monte. In snowy conditions he set top-ten stage times on some sections.

Lionel Abbott (33) leading Rob Hall in the Donington Park Fiesta Challenge race, 1982. This was Abbott Racing's opening season in motorsport. Their first victory came at the Nurburgring (Round 6) and they outscored all competitors thereafter, finishing as runners-up to Hall for the Championship. They won at Donington when Hall passed them only to have his coil lead come loose. (Abbott Racing photos)

Above: The Ford Credit Fiesta Championship has consistently produced full grids and close and exciting racing. This is a longer-than-usual race, the 100-mile event at Oulton Park in 1987.

Below: Motorcraft, the Ford-brand parts operation, sponsored this XR2 to be driven in the 1985 championship by several media celebrities, one of the ways in which publicity for the series was stimulated.

1987 Halford's Birmingham Super Prix meeting, Redex Ford Fiesta race.
Above: Simon Jones out of shape at Redex corner with the Elite Motor Sports entry.
Below: Stuart McCrudden about to spin in the Marley Foam car.
(Ian Wagstaff photos)

Above: In Germany, there were Fiesta Cup races for ladies. This is Mercedes Stermitz from Graz in Austria.

Below: This is the cockpit of a competition-prepared XR2i, retaining the standard trim but fitted with a full roll cage. The XR2i has taken over from the earlier car in one-model racing.

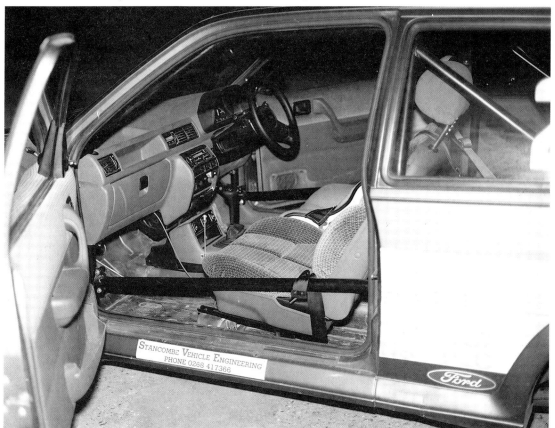

So while the XR2 no doubt benefited from technical lessons learnt in competition, it would not feature in the front line of Ford's motorsport programme. There were, and are, Fiesta-based competition machines, in rallycross for example, and club racing, but they often had only very tenuous links with the road-going specification. In branches of the sport calling for closer-to-production specifications, the Escort Mk3 soon largely took over, versions like the RS1600i and RS Turbo getting the 'right bits' homologated to compete with other manufacturers' cars in the class.

There was one area, though, where the XR2 had a long and keenly-followed competition career, and that was in the one-model racing championships which Ford promoted and for which those 1,600cc Fiestas had first been allowed out of Boreham's secret confines. One-model racing with the Mk1 and Mk2 Escort, in both 1,300cc Sport and 1,600cc Mexico forms, had been successful, but by the late 1970s those models were at the end of their production life. The first Fiesta race series was run in 1980, the competitions department at Boreham providing participants with a package of the components required to build a suitable car. It took a bit of time to get the specification sorted out, and there were handling problems, and not many competitors, in that first year. But thereafter things began to pick up. Stuart McCrudden (himself a former Mexico racer) was appointed to oversee the organisation of the championship and work on sponsorship and publicity. Backing came from *Popular Motoring*, later from the *Daily Mirror*, and, from 1983 onwards, from the Ford finance operation, Ford Credit.

With the regulations formulated to control costs by permitting only limited modification, and carefully policed to ensure fair competition, and with attractive prize funds and plenty of publicity, the Fiesta Championship grew in popularity. Stability in the rules was important, too, with everyone given plenty of notice of impending changes. For 1984, the revised car with CVH engine and five-speed gearbox was admitted to race alongside the original version, taking over completely in 1985. Evenly matched cars ensured close and hectic racing, exciting for drivers and spectators alike. By 1988, there were around 60 cars being entered, necessitating two races at many meetings.

It all made the Fiesta Championship one of the most successful forms of 'junior league' motorsport. It provided drivers with an apprenticeship in saloon-car racing rather as Formula Ford did in the single-seater sphere, and Steve Soper was just one Fiesta journeyman who went on to a top-level professional career, driving a Sierra RS Cosworth in the European and World Touring Car Championships.

For 1989, the XR2i became the chosen vehicle, with backing for the championship from another Ford subdivision, Ford Audio. Many regular competitors switched to the new car and the series looked all set to continue with unabated vigour. Those who wanted to go on racing the older car were catered for by the St Helens XR2 championship, a good form of lower-budget competition. One way and another, full grids of Fiestas jostling doorhandle-to-doorhandle for the racing line are likely to go on being a feature of British race meetings for a good while yet.

Ford Audio Fiesta Trophy action at Donington, July 1990…

…full grids of Fiestas jostling for the racing line are likely to be a feature of British racing for a long while yet.
(Ian Shaw photos)

Specifications: Ford Fiesta XR2 1981-1984

BODY

Fiesta three-door hatchback bodyshell, integral pressed-steel construction, additional wheelarch extensions and spoilers in plastic. Optional sunroof.

ENGINE

Kent series four-cylinder in-line, transverse mounting, cast iron cylinder block and head, pushrod-operated overhead valves

Bore and stroke: 80.97mm x 77.62mm.

Capacity: 1,598cc (97.6cu in).

Compression ratio: 9: 1.

Carburettor: Weber 32/34 DFT twin-choke.

Maximum power: 84bhp at 5,500rpm.

Maximum torque: 91lb/ft at 2,800rpm.

TRANSMISSION

Cable-operated single-plate clutch, diameter 200mm. Transverse four-speed gearbox.

Ratios: First 3.15: 1, second 1.91: 1, third 1.27: 1, fourth 0.95: 1, reverse 3.61: 1. Final drive ratio 3.58: 1.

Overall Gearing: 18.45mph per 1,000rpm in fourth.

SUSPENSION

Front: MacPherson struts, coil springs, transverse lower arms and tie rods.

Rear: Beam axle, trailing links, Panhard rod, telescopic dampers, anti-roll bar, coil springs.

STEERING

Rack-and-pinion, 3 turns lock-to-lock (ratio as standard Fiesta but lock restricted for wider tyres).

BRAKES

Ventilated front discs, diameter 240mm (9.4in). Rear drums, diameter 178mm (7in). Vacuum servo, dual-circuit hydraulic system.

WHEELS AND TYRES

Light alloy 6J x 13in wheels standard, tyre size 185/60 HR 13.

DIMENSIONS

Length 3,718mm (146.4in), width 1,580mm (62.2in), height 1,370mm (54in), wheelbase 2,290mm (90in), front track 1,350mm (53.1in), rear track 1,337mm (52.6in), weight 800kg (1,764lb).

PERFORMANCE

Maximum speed 105mph; 0-60mph 9.4 seconds; Fuel consumption 28-30mpg.

Specifications: Ford Fiesta XR2 1984-1989

BODY	Fiesta three-door hatchback bodyshell, restyled nose, integral pressed steel construction, additional wheelarch and sill extensions and spoilers in plastic. Optional sunroof.
ENGINE	CVH four-cylinder in-line, transverse mounting, cast iron cylinder block and light alloy head, belt-driven single overhead camshaft, hydraulic tappets.
Bore and stroke:	79.96mm x 79.52mm.
Capacity:	1,596cc (97.4cu in).
Compression ratio:	9.5: 1.
Carburettor:	Weber 32/34 DFT twin-choke.
Maximum power:	96bhp at 6,000rpm.
Maximum torque	98lb/ft at 4,000rpm.
TRANSMISSION	Cable-operated single-plate clutch, diameter 200mm. Transverse five-speed gearbox.
Ratios:	First 3.15: 1, second 1.91: 1, third 1.27: 1, fourth 0.95: 1, fifth 0.76: 1, reverse 3.61: 1. Final drive ratio 3.58: 1.
Overall gearing:	22.9mph per 1,000rpm in fifth.
SUSPENSION	
Front:	MacPherson struts, coil springs, transverse lower arms and tie rods.
Rear:	Beam axle, trailing links, Panhard rod, telescopic dampers, anti-roll bar, coil springs.
STEERING	Rack-and-pinion, 3 turns lock-to-lock (ratio as standard Fiesta but lock restricted for wider tyres).
BRAKES	Ventilated front discs, diameter 240mm (9.4in). Rear drums, diameter 178mm (7in). Vacuum servo, dual-circuit hydraulic system.
WHEELS AND TYRES	6J x 13in wheels: steel standard, with glass-reinforced plastic trim discs; light alloy optional. Tyre size 185/60 HR 13.
DIMENSIONS	Length 3,712mm (146.1in), width 1,620mm (63.8in), height 1,335mm (52.6in), wheelbase 2,290mm (90in), front track 1,385mm (54.5in), rear track 1,340mm (52.8in), weight 840kg (1,852lb).
PERFORMANCE	Maximum speed 110mph; 0-60mph 9.3 seconds; Fuel consumption 32-34mpg.

Specifications: Ford Fiesta XR2i from 1989

BODY	New-generation Fiesta three-door hatchback bodyshell, integral pressed-steel construction, additional wheelarch and sill extensions, front and rear bumper/valances and spoilers in plastic. Sunroof standard.
ENGINE	EFI development of CVH, four-cylinder in-line, transverse mounting, cast iron cylinder block and light alloy head, belt-driven single overhead camshaft, hydraulic tappets.
Bore and stroke:	79.96mm x 79.52mm.
Capacity:	1,596cc (97.4cu in).
Compression ratio:	9.75: 1.
	Multi-coil distributor-less ignition and Weber fuel injectors controlled by Ford EEC IV electronic engine management.
Maximum power:	110bhp at 6,000rpm.
Maximum torque:	102lb/ft at 2,800rpm.
TRANSMISSION	Cable-operated single-plate clutch, diameter 200mm. Transverse five-speed gearbox.
Ratios:	First 3.15: 1, second 1.91: 1, third 1.27: 1, fourth 0.95: 1, fifth 0.76: 1, reverse 3.61: 1. Final drive ratio 4.06: 1.
Overall gearing:	20.3mph per 1,000rpm in fifth.
SUSPENSION	
Front:	MacPherson struts, coil springs, lower wishbones, anti-roll bar.
Rear:	Semi-independent torsion beam, telescopic dampers, anti-roll bar, coil springs.
STEERING	Rack-and-pinion, 4.2 turns lock-to-lock.
BRAKES	Ventilated front discs, diameter 240mm (9.4in). Rear drums, diameter 203mm (8in). Vacuum servo, dual-circuit hydraulic system. Optional SCS anti-lock system.
WHEELS AND TYRES	5.5J x 13in wheels, steel standard, light alloy optional. Tyre size 185/60 HR 13.
DIMENSIONS	Length 3,743mm (147.4in), width 1,854mm (73in), height 1,320mm (52in), wheelbase 2,446mm (96.3in), front track 1,407mm (55.4in), rear track 1,377mm (54.2in), weight 910kg (2,006lb).
PERFORMANCE	Maximum speed 119mph; 0-60mph 9.0 seconds; Fuel consumption 30-32mpg.

Left: Club coup. This XR2i racer attracted wide attention at the XROC National Day in June 1989, when few people would have seen the standard version, about to go on sale. (XROC photos)

Right: Club member Gary Kay's XR2 Mk1 sits alongside the limited edition Fiesta Supersport. (Gary Kay photo)

The XR Owners Club

Whatever one's particular interest or hobby, it is always made that much more rewarding if one can share it with others. Car enthusiasts are well looked after in this respect, with clubs throughout the country catering to marques and models of all eras and offering a wide range of benefits.

The XR Owners Club was formed in 1983 'to bring together the many XR enthusiasts who share the same passion for this truly remarkable range of cars'. Since then, it has grown to a membership of more than 2,200, of which approximately 55% are XR2 or XR2i owners.

The larger the club, of course, the more it can provide in the way of services to its members. The XR Owners Club has many such advantages, ranging from free advertising in its bi-monthly magazine, *EXTRA*, to competitions, technical advice, dealer discounts, club merchandise, insurance schemes and outings such as visits to race circuits where members can profit from advanced driving instruction and the opportunity to take their cars on to the track.

The club's several regional branches offer a variety of social events. Reports in recent issues of *EXTRA* reveal fund-raising activities (including treasure hunts and a raft race!), local concours, barbecues and other happenings, plus regular 'pub meets' which members in the vicinity can attend without having to clock up expensive and time-consuming mileage.

The most eagerly awaited event of the club year is the National Day, where upwards of 300 cars gather and concours awards are keenly contested. (In that dryest of summers, 1990, it rained, but members' spirits remained undampened, even those of concours entrants obliged to devote considerable time and energy to re-cleaning their cars between showers!)

The illustrations on these pages will give some idea of the enjoyment and the perks of club-organised activities. Perhaps more important, though, are the less visible advantages of membership: the chance to learn from other owners' experiences, to talk over problems, compare notes and generally further one's knowledge of and pleasure in one's car. Add to this the savings on goods and services, and the modest enrollment and renewal fees make sound sense.

- ✳ BI-MONTHLY MAGAZINE
- ✳ CLUB INSURANCE SCHEME
- ✳ DEALER DISCOUNTS
- ✳ EXCLUSIVE XR MERCHANDISE LEISURE WEAR & ACCESSORIES
- ✳ REGIONAL BRANCH MEETINGS
- ✳ COMPETITIONS

send S.A.E. (9"x6 1/4" min) for details
XR OWNERS CLUB
PO Box 47, Loughborough, Leicestershire, LE11 1XS

This page: For some, National Day means hard work and the chance of an award. For others, it is a time to relax, watch and admire. (XROC photos)

Fiestas in print

Although this is the first book devoted exclusively to the XR2 and XR2i models, there have been a few earlier Fiesta books which make interesting reading. The first two titles described below are out of print, but might still be found in second-hand bookshops or at autojumbles, or can be borrowed from public libraries.

LET'S CALL IT FIESTA. *Edouard Seidler.* Written by an author who had Ford's full co-operation in describing how 'Project Bobcat' was begun and developed, culminating in the Fiesta's first appearance and the reactions of press and public. *Patrick Stephens, 1976.*

XR: THE PERFORMANCE FORDS. *Jeremy Walton.* This book covers the XR2 Mk1 and Mk2 in Walton's typically lively and knowledgeable style. It also includes the Escort XR3, Sierra XR4i and Sierra XR4x4. Specifications and driving impressions are provided, as well as an interesting look behind the scenes at design and engineering. *Motor Racing Publications, 1985.*

ESCORT III & CVH ENGINE TUNING MANUAL. *C.A. Bomford & K.L. Dodman.* Based on professional experience, this is a concise but reliable practical guide to upgrading CVH-engined Fords, whether for a small

increase in performance on the road or up to competition level. *BD Associates, 1987; reprinted by Bookspeed, 1990.*

THE FIESTA. *Graham Robson.* A magazine-style publication with text covering history, racing, comparisons with rivals etc., and a good range of mono and colour illustrations. *Fast Ford/Stuart McCrudden Associates, 1989.*

IMPROVE & MODIFY FIESTA (INCLUDING XR2). *Lindsay Porter & Dave Pollard.* Step-by-step instructions for DIY owners on improving the appearance, comfort or performance of the

Fiesta, accompanied by several hundred illustrations and a brief view of the cars' development history. *Haynes Publishing Group, 1990.*

There are two monthly magazines about Fords. Both contain frequent articles on Fiestas, together with display and classified advertising, industry and product news, and technical advice.

FAST FORD, A & S Publishing Co. Ltd., Central House, 154-162 Southgate Street, Gloucester GL1 2EX.
PERFORMANCE FORD, P.O. Box 14, Hazel Grove, Stockport, Cheshire SK7 6HL.

ONLY ONE MAGAZINE DIGS DEEPLY ENOUGH TO BE ABLE TO TELL YOU WHAT IS REALLY GOING ON IN THE WORLD OF FORD CARS

STANDARD OR MODIFIED, IF IT IS A FORD THEN

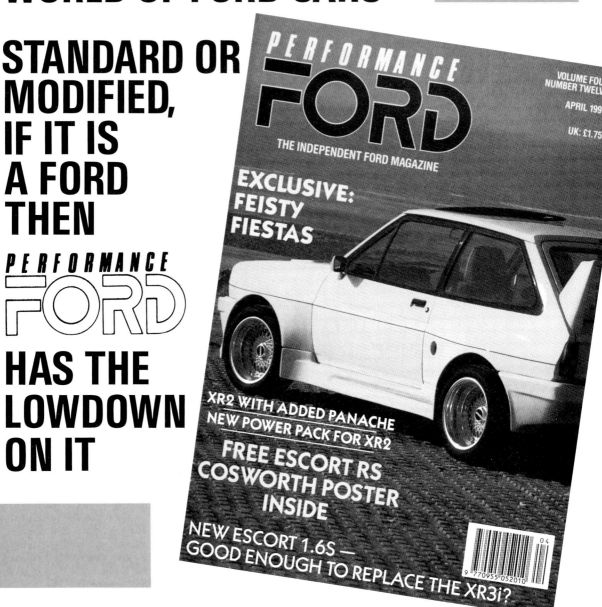

PERFORMANCE FORD

HAS THE LOWDOWN ON IT

PERFORMANCE FORD

THE INDEPENDENT FORD MAGAZINE

VOLUME FOUR
NUMBER TWELVE

APRIL 1991

UK: £1.75

EXCLUSIVE: FEISTY FIESTAS

XR2 WITH ADDED PANACHE
NEW POWER PACK FOR XR2

FREE ESCORT RS COSWORTH POSTER INSIDE

NEW ESCORT 1.6S — GOOD ENOUGH TO REPLACE THE XR3i?

9 770955 052010   04

AT A NEWSAGENT NEAR TO YOU EVERY MONTH